CONVERSATIONS WITH GOD
A DIRECT LINE TO DELIVERANCE

Outskirts Press, Inc.
Denver, Colorado

The opinions expressed in this manuscript are solely the opinions of the author and do not represent the opinions or thoughts of the publisher. The author has represented and warranted full ownership and/or legal right to publish all the materials in this book.

Conversations with God
a direct line to deliverance
All Rights Reserved.
Copyright © 2008 Olivia Crump
V2.0R1.1

Cover Photo © 2008 JupiterImages Corporation. All rights reserved - used with permission.

This book may not be reproduced, transmitted, or stored in whole or in part by any means, including graphic, electronic, or mechanical without the express written consent of the publisher except in the case of brief quotations embodied in critical articles and reviews.

Outskirts Press, Inc.
http://www.outskirtspress.com

ISBN: 978-1-4327-3100-7

Outskirts Press and the "OP" logo are trademarks belonging to Outskirts Press, Inc.

PRINTED IN THE UNITED STATES OF AMERICA

Dedication

I dedicate this book to the loving memory of my grandparents, Mr. and Mrs. Bishop Knox, my father, John Emmitt Jackson, my grandfather, Pastor Roosevelt Jackson, and my aunt, Minnie Lou Irving.

Acknowledgements

Above all, I thank God for the opportunity to help someone. I am thankful to so many people for their love, prayers, and support. My husband and children are my main source of support.

My loving husband encouraged me to share my testimony to help others. My experiences are surrounded by situations and circumstances that are rarely addressed. I appreciate him for recognizing the message in my struggles and embracing my calling, thereby giving me the courage to reach out to hurting souls.

My children are a major blessing in my life. They are bundles of inspiration to remind me there is a God. They have given me hope for each passing day I felt I would not make it. But by the grace of God through them, I am a living testimony.

Getting started was a challenge, but my mother was the spark I needed to put my voice into words. She is the inspiration behind the title, "Conversations with God". She continues to be the rock I need. Without her, I could not write this book.

My father is a minister and a believer of second chances. His input was a very important part of my book. My father is a minister and he is a believer of second chances, I was able to relax, knowing God was in control as I preceded to tell of God's deliverance.

And a many thanks to my Pastor, who helped me tremendously. I appreciate his encouragement and input in making my book flow to its perfection.

I have friends and acquaintances, who availed themselves to help in any way, providing support and prayers for me.

Preface

Often life brings about situations that are very difficult, almost breathtaking. Even with a spiritual background we find ourselves in despair, lending an ear to Satan. Deception is the strongest weapon used by the evil one. In writing this book, I am giving my testimony to let others know that God can and will deliver you from evil.

A simple conversation with God everyday will help you to make wise choices. In spite of all that may attack you, talk to Him and establish a personal relationship. Sometimes it appears that God is not listening, when in fact, those are the times He has already worked it out. I am reaching out to those who have given up hope. No situation is impossible for God.

I had given up and wanted to die but God had other plans. With the bad choices I made in life I didn't feel like I could be helped, not even by God. I was inspired to write this book to expose Satan and his evil acts in deceiving people to turn away from God and ultimately destroy their lives. Also, I am sending a message out to those who don't know God at all. It is my prayer after reading this book, you will accept God into your life and place your trust in Him. Together, we can create a domino effect, each one reach one, telling our stories to help deliver someone else.

Table of Contents

Part I 1
Genesis of Life....

Part II 7
Valley Low...

Part III 11
Forbidden...

Part IV 15
Stained Cloth...

Part V 19
Hills to Climb...

Part VI 25
Wilderness...

Part VII 29
New beginnings...

Part VIII 33
A tribute to Mama...

A message from the author 35

The following events are based on a true story, but names of people and places have been changed to protect identity.

Part I

Genesis of Life

In the beginning God...Genesis 1:1 KJV

As I reflect back to my roots, it would appear to be clear of God's plan for my life. I was predestined for ministry. When Satan heard the news, he began to set traps along the way in an attempt to terminate God's purpose for my life, but a plan delayed is not a plan denied.

Parents have an influence on the lives of their offspring. My total world as a child was focused on God, family, and church. Of course, school was at home, church and with family, as with inter-world experiences. Happily reared in a Christian family, I was well acquainted with church etiquette, Christianity and a love for God. My wholesome family setting was always: God first, others second and self last. My grandparents and parents consisted of Pastors, Ministers, Evangelists, Teachers, Church Mothers, Deacons, and Missionaries, with only one sibling, my brother Lamar, who had somehow gone astray. He was considered the "black sheep" of the family. I often wondered, what happened to cause such a separation. Now I am praying God brings him back to his roots.

My grandmother was the backbone of my family, the inspiration we needed to pull through the rough times. She was the church mother at True Way Healing Temple, where she was highly respected by everyone. Her teachings to the young women went down in history. She was courageous, but meek as a dove. I am a living testimony of her prayers and devotion to God. During my high school years, I suffered the loss of both grandfathers, and my father. These men were mighty warriors with a legacy that produced inspiring doctors, lawyers, judges, educators, ministers, entrepreneurs, authors, mothers, and fathers.

A few years passed and my mother, Lillie Hill became

acquainted with a man, Reverend Monroe Jacobs, Pastor of Throne of Mercy Holiness Church. Later, they were married and I had a new father. At first, I had a difficult time accepting him, because of the memory in my heart of my father. But as time went on, I realized that God blessed me with another father that portrayed all the qualities of the three powerful men that were in my life, my grandfathers and my father all rolled into one. Now I did not have to worry, my mother was not alone and she was happy.

Going off to college was an unforgettable experience. I met my husband John Stuart at University of Pine Valley. I fell in love with John, because he was so different from anyone I knew. I was attracted to his forbidden candor. I wanted so desperately to acquaint myself with something outside a spiritual rim. I had to escape and explore all that I missed. John and I were wed in 1987 at True Way Healing Temple, where I grew as a child. This was also the year I became a mother. Our struggles were endless. I was a young mother and a new wife with hopes and dreams for my new family, but there were many nights I cried myself to sleep not knowing how we would make it from one day to the next. My idea of family was destroyed. I was estranged from my family; I had no one. The thought of telling anyone of my sadness sealed my silence.

I remember one Christmas, I decided instead of sending my daughter Dorcas to church I would go also. I had hoped John would go with us, but he refused. He promised to spend the rest of the day with us after church. This pleased me because Christmas was my favorite holiday and John was not spending much time at home.

So, off to church Dorcas and I went. My cousin, Evelyn came by to give us a ride. Service was beautiful and I knew the rest of the day would be too. Dorcas had gifts to open and John was waiting to have a special Christmas with us. My mother invited us to her house for dinner, but I knew John, Dorcas and I needed this time to bond. Finally we arrived home, but much to my surprise, John wasn't there. Maybe he went out for some air or maybe he's getting some Christmas dinner, I thought to myself. Perhaps, his mother Nadine was sending plates for us. She always cooked more and gave it to us. So I waited and waited until I realized how late it was. Dorcas and I opened the gifts. We did not have much, but she was so happy with the toys and games. Time went on and before I knew it, Dorcas and I had spent Christmas without John. Night came and I put Dorcas to bed. Very late that night, John came home. Even though I knew there could not possibly be an excuse for his absence, I wanted so badly for there to be one. And then it came, he was at the gym playing basketball with his friends. I had always known that he did not love me enough to be there for me, but I hoped he loved Dorcas enough to at least share Christmas with us. This would be one of many days that we were last on John's mind. We had very hard times and I was too embarrassed to ask my family for help. John's family labeled me an unfit mother because of the hidden issues in our marriage; often we did not have enough diapers or food for Dorcas. They didn't know the whole story; they were looking in from the outside. Most of the financial aid came from his family, and they blamed me for all the poverty difficulty, according to John.

One cold night our utilities had been shut off; we had plans to receive assistance the next morning, but needed to get through the night. John decided to call his mother and ask if we could stay the night with her. Nadine's answer was Dorcas and John could come, but I was not welcome. John's response was if all of us couldn't come, then nobody would. Then he hung up the phone. Our apartment was extremely cold and I had to get my baby out of there. I did what any mother would have done. I told John to call Nadine back and accept the invitation to her house and I would stay home. I could tell this did not please him. He could not believe his mother would turn me away. He learned something that night. It was that I was determined to keep our family going. John and Dorcas left and there I was alone in that cold dark place of emptiness with nothing but my thoughts. Several minutes later, the phone rang; it was John's grandmother Emma, who lived across the street in an elderly community. I guess she talked to John and knew I was left behind, but made no mention of that. She simply extended an invitation for me to come to her house that night. With tears in my eyes, I accepted. She knew my pain, but did not utter a word, Emma just showed me love and I will remember that for the rest of my days. I was hurting inside and I kept it to myself. My focus was on being a good mother and trying to hold my family

3

together for Dorcas.

In 1992, we had another beautiful baby girl. We named her Ashley Mariah. Some years had passed by now and it seemed my family would make it after all. John was working a steady job and things were starting to look up. My marriage was far from perfect. But I felt now, John wanted things to work out and I was hopeful.

911-2GOD

Well God, it's me. There is no way I could have made it thus far without you. I know with all my heart this was not your plan for me, but thank you for not leaving me. Please be patient with me. Help me to be a good mother. And God, please do something special for John.

Part II

Valley Low

Yea, though I walk through the valley of the shadow of death....
Psalms 23:4 KJV

My family and I were attending Open Door Full Gospel Mission. It was quite intimate and very family oriented. For the first time in my marriage, I felt as if rough days were behind us. My husband, John became involved in ministry and things were good. An old acquaintance, Bertha, invited us to Open Door one Sunday morning. I didn't know at that time this was part of Satan's plan. I didn't expect him to attack in an invitation to church. But when you have people in your life praying for you, Satan needs strategy. After a few visits, John and I decided to join. The families in our church were very close because we were small in numbers. I wanted so desperately to reunite with my parents, but I needed more time to put my life back on track. I didn't want them to know what I had gone through, for it would surely be a disappointment to them. From time to time, I would call, but for the most part I led them to believe I didn't want to be bothered. As I reflect back, I know God was with me, even though I thought I was alone.

Bertha and I were high school friends. We had gone our separate ways, but met up again years later while shopping. We were excited to see one another again. Spending several minutes catching up and of course, showing baby pictures, Bertha could sense that I was troubled. She asked me, "How are you, really?" I hesitated with my answer because she seemed so happy. And although, John and I were doing better; we had so far to go. She suggested getting together to introduce our husbands and children. I agreed, I needed someone in my life and maybe she would be the friend that I longed for. Our lives became intertwined and we spent several occasions on family outings. John liked spending time with Bertha's husband Bill. He was a minister and I liked that John had someone spiritual as a friend. I really began to have faith that God was going to mend our marriage and everything would be alright.

Bertha prayed with me and she understood my troubles. She accepted me, flaws and all. I could be myself with her and she yet wanted our friendship. For the first time in years, I was able to open up to someone and release feelings of anguish I had bottled inside. We had many talks sharing the joys and pain of marriage and parenting.

Bertha and Bill were concerned that John and I were not attending church anywhere. So Bertha extended us an invitation to their church, Open Door, where we later joined. John and I were doing well for awhile, but that changed and my worst nightmare began to be a reality. John started slipping back to his old way. "My God, I cannot go through this again," I would pray and cry until I could not cry anymore.

I began to notice that our money was low and nothing to account for it. Checks were bouncing and there were several withdrawals from our account. I confronted John, but he would manage to turn the tables with me apologizing to him. I loved him so much and wanted to believe in him. But something was wrong and I did not know how to fix it. All I knew was we had two daughters that depended on us. Finally after several confrontations, John told me he had a gambling problem. He promised to get help, but also felt he could do it on his own. Since we belong to a church now, I thought, maybe we can finally get the help needed to put our marriage together. So John and I agreed to seek pastoral counseling with our Pastor, Reverend Herman Blackstone.

The counseling seemed to be going quite well. John had grown fond of Pastor Blackstone; he was so understanding and sensitive to our needs. Up to now, John really did not trust anyone with the details of his addiction, not even me. I felt this was truly a breakthrough for our family. John and I trusted Pastor Blackstone and we held him in high esteem. As time passed, John confided in Pastor about his father leaving when he was a young boy. So much emotion went into this story; I could hardly keep dry eyes. Pastor Blackstone filled a void for John as the father he so desired, and we continued the counseling.

After a year or so, John's father, Ralph phoned him. Emotions were overflowing because John had not seen his father in many years. The reunion was a strain on John, but his desire was for Ralph to meet Dorcas and Ashley. John and his father began to bond. Shortly after, Ralph was stricken with a heart attack. John later learned that Ralph died in a crack house. Devastation overtook John and he displayed unexplainable reactions with a forcible desire to imitate the bad conduct of his father. This caused our household to be in a valley so low, it would take every ounce of energy I had to keep our family going. I was married, but alone and a single parent.

Ashley was older now and I was working part time; however, weeks later, my family was lacking transportation. Pastor Blackstone so generously offered to give us a helping hand. During many rides, much conversation took place. He was so attentive to whatever I had to say. He often made reference to my being deprived of a listening ear. Reverend Blackstone was our transportation to and from church, work, and any errands that were needed. "Oh what a giving person," I thought on many occasions. And for the most part, I believe those were his intentions.

One day, when John wasn't home, Pastor Blackstone phoned him. After telling Pastor he wasn't home, he continued to talk to me. I could hear the anguish in his voice, so I asked him to tell me what had him sounding so down. He answered with a long sigh, telling me of his bad marital situation. He talked as if he had no one and I knew I had nothing to offer as I listened. I also shared with him the ups, mostly downs to my marriage. When I ended the call, I felt strange. I felt a transferring of spirits through that experience. I would not share this with anyone at that time because I was frightened of the weight of this information. A seed was planted that day and Satan used my fear to keep me silent. I went on, although I knew this wasn't the end.

911-2GOD

Oh Dear God, Is Pastor Blackstone the man I thought him to be? I know he's not perfect, just as I am not. So, why do I feel this way? Did I make a mistake trusting him? Please show me. Please protect my family and me.

Part III

Forbidden

>...Touch it, lest ye die. Genesis 3:3 KJV

There was a knock at my door. I wasn't expecting anyone, but my instinct told me who would be on the other side of that door. I answered and Pastor Blackstone came in. My eyes were surprised to see him, but my spirit was expecting him. I knew from that day, I had gone to a forbidden point and I wasn't sure if I could return. Before I could say a word, we were sharing a passionate kiss. I didn't know why, it wasn't something that I wanted, I loved my husband. But there I was, kissing the Pastor of our church, a place where I thought my family and I would have a fresh start. All respect for the church and men of the cloth I cherished all of my life was diminished. I couldn't believe I was traveling this road. Something inside me danced to the music of his harp. I was unable to help myself and I felt silenced.

The phone calls increased by the day, during every available break that Reverend Blackstone had; he would call me. The attraction grew stronger with each passing day. I wasn't at all sure why. I felt as if I was outside my body. I was crying inside and no one could hear. I was romanced and every effort was made to sweep me away. I fell hard and this is when my life went down a spiral. I spent my nights crying about this indiscretion and my days anticipating more. What is this that ails me? I wanted to stop and I didn't want to stop. This had to be the most confusing time in my life. Why did this man pursue me? I didn't know at the time I was predestined to be a danger to Satan. I didn't know what plans God had for my life. The demonic plan was to destroy me.

A sexual encounter with this man was to say at least unusual and mystical. I did not have enough strength to say no, but I knew that it was wrong. I had a spiritual upbringing and endless knowledge of demonic persuasion and possession. "For we wrestle not against flesh and blood, but against principalities, against powers, against the rulers of the darkness of this world, against spiritual wickedness in high places" (Ephesians 6:12 KJV). But still I remained silent.

Cries of a silent frustration, I wanted so desperately to turn back the hands of time as I sank deeper in this love affair. Finally, I decided to confide in Bertha. I believed she would understand and pray to help me find my way back to what I've always known. After I poured out my soul, Bertha turned on me; she took the information and called an emergency church meeting. All that I had shared with her was exposed for all to see. Open Doors Full Gospel Mission did not survive, the doors eventually closed. At this point, I felt a mixture of things, but guilt was dominant. I began to feel obligated to help rebuild and all was forgiven by Pastor Blackstone. This was another evil device of Satan to keep me entrapped in this relationship. Reverend Blackstone started services again at a new location, which was Kid Kountry Daycare during normal business hours. I hated Pastor Blackstone for what I had become and I hated Mrs. Blackstone because she was weak and defenseless, but in my heart I knew she was a victim also. I could not separate myself from Satan's evil acts. There we were sitting there Sunday after Sunday supporting this man and damned to hell; we were on our way. What happened? Why couldn't I make intelligent decisions anymore? Why was my spouse so blind? I didn't want John to know what was going on with me, but there were times I did want him to know, so he could help me. But John had issues of his own.

I struggled to keep my marriage from being victimized by this demonic relationship between our Pastor and me. John was dealing with some strong holds of his own. He had struggles with outside influences, which focused his attention elsewhere, therefore unknowingly aiding me in keeping this affair a secret. I still wanted my marriage, but I was losing all that I knew and I did not know which way to turn.

In 1995, I gave birth to a son. We named him James Christopher. By now, my secrets had piled so high, I could not breathe. Pastor Blackstone tormented me everyday with the possibility of James being his son, John was elated to finally have a son and the mere thought of James not being his child made me physically ill. Later a private test proved he had no claim to my baby boy. I could not continue this way; I had a war going on inside me. I had turned away from God. I was cut off from my family and my husband was locked in a demonic world of his own.

John was falling deeper into drugs and I was accepting money from Herman to keep the household going; he was no longer Pastor Blackstone to me. Many nights he would come over and we would go into the drug infested neighborhoods looking for John. The search was endless. Sometimes we were successful and in some instances, we did not have a clue. I despised Reverend Blackstone, but I was deceived into believing he was all I had. I wanted to tell John's mother; I struggled with this for a long time and John's addictions were getting worse. Finally after John was missing for about a week, I called Nadine. After hearing my story about her son, she came over immediately. Nadine arrived at my home in total disarray. She was speechless; I did not know how to comfort her, before now our relationship was solely about the children. I did not feel any animosity towards her. I felt empathy because I understood her pain. I had no answer for any of this. Our holes were too deep. I did not know what would become of us. I stopped talking to the Lord and I didn't allow myself to hear from Him either.

911-2GOD

DISCONNECTED

Part IV

Stained Cloth

...Come out of the man, thou unclean spirit. Mark 5:8 KJV

Depending on Reverend Blackstone became a lifestyle for me. He supported me financially and my children bonded with him. One day when Dorcas returned home from school, the reverend came over for a casual visit. I was cooking and Dorcas was doing her homework. She needed help with a particular assignment in a subject I didn't understand. Reverend Blackstone offered to help while I finished dinner. I happened to walk across the hall and out of my peripheral vision, I thought I saw something. Instantly I convinced myself I was imagining things. So I went on, but the thought was still in my mind. Reverend Blackstone left and I went to see if Dorcas was about finished with her homework, but I saw something so disturbing to me. My heart stopped, as I looked at her. I noticed she wasn't wearing panties. I asked why. The answer Dorcas gave me took my breath away! The wind was knocked totally from me! She said Reverend Blackstone told her to remove her panties. Looking at her, I knew she didn't understand why; she was an innocent little girl. With a knot in my throat, I asked, "What did he do?" Dorcas responded by saying, "He touched me." With every ounce of air I could muster, I asked, "What else did he do?" As I held my breath, she answered, "Nothing." At this point, I felt relief and rage in the same hot moment. It was now I must ask my parents for help because now Satan had gone too far. This was the hardest thing for me to do. I wanted to die and that day I believe I did.

Many prayers and support went up for me. I couldn't pray for myself. My family interceded on my behalf. An account of this evil relationship would be about five years. I survived this horrific event in my life, but there are yet countless of others dealing with sexual sins. Don't be silent; exposure leads to the road of deliverance. My now former Pastor sought help for sexual sins of the flesh because he was exposed. He later revealed he was a "peeping tom" as a child. Also as an adult, he had thoughts and sexual fantasies involving his own children. Sex demons are responsible for the lust that leads to sex sins. They rank high in the hierarchy of demons. Lust is the third of the seven deadly sins. "Howbeit this kind goeth not out but by prayer and fasting" (St. Matthew 17:21 KJV).

911-2GOD

Oh God! I have been in bondage for so long, my soul cries out to thee. Thank you for my deliverance! You protected my children. You were there all the time. Oh dear God, John is still lost. Please help him.

Part V

Hills to Climb

> I will lift mine eyes unto the hills…Psalms 121:1 KJV

My parents and mother-in-law helped me through some really rough episodes. Many days, I wrestled with whether I should just pack up, take my children and leave my husband, but somehow I found strength to make it one more day. John became a functional addict. He would work a normal work week and on weekends, he would disappear. I was exhausted trying to keep up with his whereabouts. I finally gave him an ultimatum; get some help or lose his family for good. We were attending church with my parents at Throne of Mercy Holiness Church. John seemed to really want to change, but he was uncomfortable attending church with my family. I really believe that Satan was afraid if we continued there, John would be delivered, but I was committed to making our marriage work, so we eventually left Throne of Mercy.

John and I joined a community outreach ministry. John was still at battle with his addictions, but he wanted help now. He finally realized he would lose everything if things didn't change. The Pastor of this ministry had a testimony of being delivered from drugs so he related to John's constant struggle with cocaine. I would have rather been at Throne of Mercy, but if John could be helped elsewhere, I was willing to make the move.

I became ill and for a couple of weeks I nursed what I thought to be a virus. Later, I found out I was pregnant. This was quite a surprise, my conceiving in spite of preventive measures. Even in my womb, I called this baby a miracle. I had no plans for another child, but blessed was all I felt. Something about this pregnancy made me realize that God was going to bless me to be the mother I needed to be. I was not worried. I began to take my attention off my circumstances and I focused on God, my help, my strength, my way out of no way, my Redeemer. Everyday I thanked God for being a survivor.

"Move out of the way, I got it!" I can remember John yelling at the paramedics. I remember all the shouting, the sirens going off, and being shoved into the ambulance with the best of intentions. All of this came about on the night of January 15, 1998, the eve of my fourth child's birth.

I woke up that night and called my children into my bedroom. Dorcas and Ashley were helping me to get dressed. James, my son, was too young to know what was going on. John was at work and we only tried to make do until he came home. Dorcas gathered a few items, packed my bag and called 911. It was a snow storm that night and the ambulance was delayed. John had to melt the ice from the car door lock, so he could not come right away either. The 911 operator was instructing Dorcas how to assist me until help could arrive. Finally, the paramedics arrived. They were having such a hard time getting me down the porch steps and into the ambulance. Finally, John came to the rescue. He had to leave work and I'm sure he sped all the way home. Being a big and strong man, he lifted me into the ambulance without a problem. Arriving at the hospital, I knew it was the beginning of a long night. Hours later, I gave birth to a baby boy. Our first son was the namesake of my husband, John Christopher and his twin brother, James who didn't have a son. John wanted him to share in the birth of our son. But God blessed us with another son, so we decided to name him John Samuel, the namesake of John and my stepfather, Monroe, whose middle name is Samuel.

John was trying to be a better husband and father, but evil was always present. He would make positive strides to do well and before long Satan would snatch him back. This war going on with John was devastating to watch. My parents, Nadine and I would pray continuously for John. Finally after years of being in and out of fellowship with God, John decided he no longer wanted to be a husband or a father, so he left without trace. My husband of fifteen years walked out on our four children and me. What I didn't know, God was with me all the time. He delivered me from a bad relationship, but I couldn't see beyond my pain.

Seeking assistance, I was afforded an opportunity to return to school. I enrolled in Nursing Assistant courses. This was so exciting, because I needed a livelihood to care for my children. One day while sitting in class, I began to drift back in time, when I was fourteen. My favorite aunt, Louise was terminally ill and needed 24 hour care. Often, my mother would take me to her house so I could sit with her. I assisted Aunt Louise with personal care and I even tried to cook. But all I could prepare was scrambled eggs and jello, which became her favorite meal. I loved to braid her long, beautiful, coarse hair. Aunt Louise was such an attractive lady and I admired her greatly. Before her illness, she was a Nurse's Assistant at a prominent children's hospital and loved by all her patients. She loved caring for others; she was a nurturing soul. When she died, I could still hear her tell me how much my caring for her meant. Aunt Louise inspired me to care for sick people and those that can't help themselves.

Collecting myself, while listening to my instructor, I knew I was in the right place fulfilling my purpose. Although it was unknown what was next, I knew God was in control. I passed my state exam and received my state certification as a Nurse's Assistant; this meant steady income in a field in high demand. Raising children alone wasn't easy, but God opened doors and provided for us. My family was supportive and God blessed me with Christian co-workers, who offered help and friendship.

About a year had passed now and John called. He was very apologetic and with every effort explained his actions. Although I had moved on, I still loved John and had not given up on our family reuniting. I allowed him back into our lives. An effort of trying to make our marriage work was draining. John was envious of my accomplishments. He often belittled me and many days I felt worthless. I began to question his returning because he made each day hard for me to live my life and care for our children.

We argued and fought constantly until he decided to leave again. John stayed away for a while, coming back with another attempt to reconcile with me. I know he may have had good intentions, but the back and forth of this relationship made me wary and it was unstable for the children. So I filed for divorce. The road ahead was so rough and I cried many nights. Confusion started to settle in my mind about my marriage ending. I felt I had failed my children. I began to reminisce about my past struggles. Before I knew it, depression crept back into my life.

Everyday it was business as usual, but inside I was dying. I didn't want anyone to know because in my mind this was something else to add to my list of failures. I didn't allow myself to vent and release emotions. For some reason, I always thought I needed to be strong and keep going. Divorce was so final and it was as if a family member died, and I didn't take the time to grieve. I didn't want anyone to know that after all John had taken us through, I yet loved him; I felt foolish. But there will always be a special spot in my heart for John because of our four beautiful children.

Slowly I sank into depression. Feelings of worthlessness were a part of my everyday thoughts. I started taking my mind off God and began to think about my past more and more each day. Instead of looking forward, I looked back, causing myself to go deeper. I had uncontrollable crying one day and the next recollection I have, I was riding in the back of a police car, handcuffed.

"You're going to be just fine," the officer said to me. Be just fine, I thought. "Where am I going," I asked. "To the hospital," he answered. When we arrived at the hospital, the officer told me I seemed like such a nice young woman and he hoped I would receive the help I needed. He wished me luck and someone else helped me inside. I was taken to what looked like a jail cell. I did not remember what happened to make things end up this way, but I wasn't afraid, peace came over me. When I entered the cell, there was no one else in it. I went to the back of this small block to sit down. There was another chair in front of me and someone was sitting in it. I'm thinking to myself, I have really lost it now because this cell was empty when I came in. The lady rolled her chair to mine. She knew things about me and I didn't know how. She began to talk, quoting scriptures and reassuring me that everything would be alright.

Finally, the doctor came and when he walked in, he made no acknowledgment the other lady was there. She just stood there while the doctor talked to me. He told me the waiting room was full with my family and friends. He asked me some questions and I answered as best I could. Afterwards, he told me I did not belong at that particular facility; he believed rest was what I needed. He told me he was going to the waiting room to speak to my family. The lady was still there with me. My mother-in-law worked in this hospital and I asked to see her. Nadine came to the ward and with tears in her eyes, she asked, "What happened?" We talked and embraced and before long I was released to my family to be transported to another facility. As I walked away, still in Nadine's arms, I remembered the lady. I told Nadine I needed to go back and thank her for helping me through a difficult time, but when I did, she wasn't there. I asked the nurses about her, but they looked confused and told me I was in the cell alone. I walked away knowing, I had a guardian angel.

Upon arriving at the other hospital, I began to feel better, but my parents were very concerned and wanted to make sure I would be alright. I had endured so much and had reached a breaking point. They felt that I would benefit from therapy and I agreed. I was admitted into the hospital, where I would receive an evaluation. It was the week of Easter. God spoke to me and said this was a time of restoration for me and on Good Friday I would be going home. This was the second time I heard I needed to rest. My Pastor's wife came to visit and she told me God spoke to her and said, "restoration", a third time God spoke these words. On the second day, I was told by my doctor evaluations took approximately two weeks, but I remembered what God promised me. Later that day, I was able to talk, encourage, have prayer and plant seeds of hope with the other patients. On the third day, which was Good Friday, I walked to the nurse's station and announced I was ready to be released. The nurse looked perplexed telling me that wasn't possible. She informed me she would call my doctor. So I waited and when he arrived, I told him I was ready to go home. He stared at me as if he was trying to figure me out. He broke the silence by asking if I would agree to seek outpatient therapy. I told him I would. He signed my release papers and I was free to return home to my family. I learned from that experience. I met so many people that were in really bad situations, who had given up on life. Many didn't know God and others needed to be reminded of His grace and mercy. It was then, I realized my life is a testimony to help others.

911-2GOD

Oh God, from now on, you will be first in my life, for you have proven yourself to me time after time. I didn't understand why I endured so much pain and struggle, but I know now that my life is a testimony of deliverance. Lord, I know you have the answer to all problems and I know you didn't bring me this far to leave me now. With all the gratitude in my heart I thank you and now Lord, I am putting all my trust in you for a total sense of direction.

Part VI

In the Wilderness

And I will give her her vineyards back to thence...Hosea 2:15 KJV

Returning home from the hospital, I was uncertain about the future. I trusted God, but I wanted to be reassured that all was well. Many people have the misconception that when you become a Christian, there are no more troubles or struggles, but quite the contrary. Thinking back on what God brought me through took me to a place I didn't understand, a place where I had to seek God for my life's purpose.

I received many phone calls with kind words and prayer. But one call in particular stood out from the rest. It was peculiar. The caller was not someone I would expect to hear from. It was the brother of an old acquaintance. Years ago, I became friends with a neighbor, Pearl. I became acquainted with her family and we were involved in many activities together, mostly church functions. Even when I moved away, we still kept in touch. Pearl was like a big sister to me and when I needed an escape, I could go to her house and feel so much peace. She worried about me a lot and always wanted to know what was going on with me. She often told me she felt a deep connection to me, but didn't know why. Well Joshua, Pearl's brother, called me because he learned I was going through a difficult time and although he wasn't sure about calling me, he wanted me to know I could call him if I needed to talk. He also offered to take the children to the zoo to give me time alone. I really didn't know how to react. Nevertheless, I thanked him, gracefully turned down his offer and ended the call. Later that week, I gave Pearl a call. I wanted to know a little more about the mysterious call from her brother. With hesitation, she told me Joshua had always been my admirer. I was surprised, because my life had been such a mess. The few times we bumped into one another at Pearl's house, I was mostly in despair and wanted to talk to my big sister, so what could he possibly see in me. Anyway, I put that whole thought to rest by telling her I was not interested in dating and she understood.

During this period in life, I was pretty much a loner. I had my children, my work, and church, but I lived each day searching. I did not know exactly what I was looking for, but I knew I was supposed to be doing more. I prayed and waited for answers. I felt as if I was in a dry place. I wanted to know what was needed to fill this void. God delivered me from depression. My children were doing fine. I loved my profession of caring for the elderly. I was reunited with my family. I no longer suffered the abuse of bad relationships. So, what was missing? Shouldn't I feel whole? Waiting on an answer from God I buried myself in work.

Everyday was a busy day at the Senior Living Retirement Community...

"Good morning, it's time for breakfast. How are you today? Do you need help with your shoes? Did you remember to put in your teeth? Here, let me help you."

Down the hall as I gathered residents to get the day started, I anticipated the conversation I would have with all the seniors in my care. Working with the elderly, true enough, began as employment, but as time passed, I gained friends and before long they were my extended family. My parents, Pastor and Mrs. Monroe Jacobs began prayer services for the seniors at Senior Living. This was truly a blessing because many of the residents didn't have an opportunity to attend church. Through these visits, we formed a circle of friendship.

My life was good, but I was unable to embrace it. I believe I was afraid to move forward. I just wanted it to last. I wanted happiness for so long, now I didn't know how to enjoy it. Taking one day at a time, I prayed for direction and the wisdom to make the right choices, so I would never be in bondage again. God delivered me from life threatening situations and the thought of going backwards gave me chills. I really didn't entertain the ideal of many friends. I was always leery of any new acquaintances. So fearful of the unexpected or the unknown of new relationships and trying to remain free of people, I created a new bondage. I knew this was unhealthy, but it sure felt safe. Being a mother and a caregiver for my seniors was all I needed. I was exhausted with the mere thought of anything more.

911-2GOD

Oh God, I'm living my life in a fish bowl, because I'm afraid of getting hurt. Help me to live my life. Show me your perfect will for my life. Give me the wisdom and discernment I need to make the right choices

Part VII

New Beginnings

> …Old things are passed away; behold all things are become new. II Corinthians 5:17 KJV

One Saturday afternoon, Pearl called me. She asked if I was interested in going to a movie. I hadn't been out in a while, so I thought, why not, I probably needed a change of scenery. She placed me on hold, returning with Joshua on the other line. She told him I wanted to see a movie. I knew then, this call was a set up. I quickly thought of a way of escape, so I thought. "So, does this mean my four children can come along too," I asked Joshua. I'm thinking this would probably change his mind, but it didn't. I had forgotten our first conversation when he offered to take the children to the zoo. I was unable to frighten him away, so we all went to the movies, Pearl, Joshua, my children and me. In spite of all my efforts to not give in, I had a really nice time.

Later that evening, Joshua called and the conversation was refreshing. But I can't do this again. I would go over and over in my mind, after each call from him. The harder I tried to push him away, the harder he pushed to be in my life. I couldn't understand why he wanted to date me. I felt like damaged goods. I didn't at all see myself attracting anyone. I was divorced with four children and a past that screamed, run for your life! Joshua knew everything there was to know about me, but it didn't seem to make a difference. The mystery of his kindness took my attention off what I believed to be undesirable about myself and placed it on new beginnings.

Joshua and I dated and I had so much fun with him. He made me laugh constantly. I couldn't remember the last time I felt so alive. My children loved him, but I was afraid if I allowed myself to love again, I would be heartbroken. As much as Joshua seemed to enjoy us, surely he couldn't want more, I would think to myself. So, I decided to just enjoy the fun and happy times while they lasted.

Several months had passed and much to my surprise, Joshua was still pursuing me. Finally he asked if he could meet my parents. Well, I didn't give this much thought before, because I really didn't expect the relationship to last. This was during the holiday season, so I invited him to come to my parent's home for Christmas dinner. My family adored Joshua and he admired my parents. We dated for a few more months and I began to fall in love. Feelings I thought were locked away forever were surfacing. Joshua told me he loved me also. But even so, I didn't believe that it would be more than that, but on Valentine's Day, something happened.

Joshua came over with candy, stuffed animals, and balloons. He called the children downstairs and with excitement they flew to see what he wanted. After passing out gifts, he pulled a small box out of his pocket and asked the children to gather around. I nearly passed out when he got down on one knee. Joshua proposed marriage to me and before I could answer, the children shouted, "Yes!" All this time, I was guarding my heart, fearing Joshua didn't want more, but he wanted it all with my children and me. I cried the rest of the day with so much joy in my heart.

Planning the wedding was a very happy occasion and I savored every moment. I was on top of the world and felt nothing could bring me down. Pearl, Joshua's sister was elated during the courtship, but when she learned of the engagement, everything went sour. She was responsible for confusion among the family. Instead of being happy for me, she seemed jealous. I don't believe she expected marriage from us. I knew she was unhappy and alone. We had several talks about it, but she told me she had given it all to the Lord. She believed He would one day bless her with a husband. So when she began to act this way, I knew she was hurting about her own situation. I tried to be patient with her, but Pearl began to undermine the wedding and caused so much grief. She twisted information from my past and made up stories to add to the things she already knew about me. Joshua's family loved him so much; they trusted that he was following his heart and that everything would be alright. In spite of the lies Pearl was spreading, Joshua's happiness was their only concern. They really didn't know much about me, but they accepted my children and me into their family.

Joshua and I blissfully wed June of 2003. The first year was hard, trying to rise above the many attempts of Satan to destroy this union. Pearl had not given up. When she lost the battle of convincing her family to stop the wedding, she began to work on me. With much effort, she wanted me to believe her family hated me. Finally, I believed her and I stopped visiting my in-laws. I felt rejected and I wanted nothing to do with them. This was a strain on my marriage. Joshua put so much stock in family; he was grief stricken by my decision. Nothing he could say made me believe any different about his family. So he stopped going to family gatherings also because he didn't want to go without me. Joshua's love for me was beyond my understanding. He was determined to keep me happy; as a result, we were estranged from his family for two years.

One weekend, Joshua desired to visit his older sister, Florida. We had some confrontations in the past, but we worked through them for Joshua. We sat in her den engaging in small talk. I don't know how it started, but we went into deep discussion about the family and my relationship with them. Before now, we avoided that subject to keep peace. We began to compare notes and suddenly realized our estrangement was the result of lies. We all broke down and cried. From that moment on, I have not missed a chance to spend time with family and friends. Life is just too short and it needs to be lived to the fullest. As much as I wanted to be angry with Pearl, I understood my battle was not with her.

Satan does not care who or what he uses to carry out his evil plans. You must be watchful as well as prayerful. He will try to get as close as possible to his prey, which means his spirit will enter someone you least expect as an attack. When Satan feels threatened, he pulls out the big guns. As the older saints would say, "higher level, bigger devil"; I found this to be true. But one thing to remember, Satan has no new tricks. He gives himself away. I am able to recognize him from the pattern he set. He has always shown himself in someone close to me. As shrewd as he thinks he is, he still does not have anything new. Satan lost again.

911-2GOD

Dear God, Thank you for a second chance to love. Thank you for a wonderful man that loves my children and me unconditionally. Thank you for family and friends. Thank you for your divine favor, but most of all, thank you for my deliverance.

Part VIII
Mama

> For this child I prayed…1 Samuel 1:27 KJV

There have been many people in my life I called friends that were just passing through. I placed my trust in people I thought cared. Some people are in your life for a season, some are there for a reason, but my mama has always been there. I didn't always understand why or what was her reasoning for things, but I do know she is spirit led. I could not have been able to survive the most devastating events in my life without her prayers and support. She's believes that I am a winner.

During many days of turmoil, I did not call or visit her much, but I always felt connected. I knew my mother was praying for me because I had angels watching over me. When I became a mother, I knew what it meant to let go and give it to God. I often mistook that for her not caring. Fact is, she cared enough to step back knowing God was in control.

My mother is a strong, gifted and insightful woman. Her ways are peculiar because she is in tune with the Holy Spirit. The advice she gives comes from heaven's door. While embarking on new beginnings, I am able to listen to her with understanding now.

I often say that I am a late bloomer or I need to make up for lost time. My mom says to me, "You are in the time that God predestined for you. Things are done on his time not ours, so you're right on schedule to do what God has ordained you to do." So I'm encouraged to go and tell the good news God will deliver you from the hands of Satan. It doesn't matter how low you go, God can and will reach down to pick you up. One thing about being low, you're in the perfect position to look up.

My mother is my rock and through her I know God. I am spreading the gospel that God is the same today as He was yesterday. What He did for me, He will do the same for you.

911-2GOD

Well God, mother knew best, for in her womb you chose me. She prayed and didn't worry, because she knew you would do the rest.

A message from the author...

My Testimony

... And by the word of their testimony... Revelation 12:11 KJV

The best of me is hidden within. My soul cries silently; no one can hear the silent frustration. I search trying to find something to fill this void....

Years of searching, the answer was inside me. It was trying to get out, but was trapped by my circumstances. All the heartache and pain of my inner being longing to be released was caged and labeled depression. This was my life.

Situations had me buried so far under, I did not remember life any other way. I had been tossed about and I felt nothing. Depression was an escape. I made myself numb by training myself not to feel or react. I knew God, but I didn't want Him to deliver me, because that would mean to live again. The thought of that terrified me. To live was to hurt, but God had other plans. He had invested something inside me no matter what, I could feel his presence. I sought counseling with my Pastor at that time, which ended in a love affair. My trust and love for the church waxed cold. I sank deeper. I was buried so deep, I knew I could not come out. I was convinced I was lost forever. I once knew the Lord, I accepted Him into my life as a child. But surely, I sank so low, Jesus couldn't pick me up. Not after I left him and refused his help. What I didn't know, God was with me all the time,

I didn't want to seek him fearing it would unlock my soul. Being in bondage was a lifestyle I had grown accustom. I hear God along this journey, but I say to myself, these are voices from my pain. Maybe, if I medicate myself, the voices will go away. I tried so hard to lose myself, but nothing eased my pain. Although I had been estranged from my family, I knew someone was praying for me, even though, I had given up and I knew I wanted to die.

My husband of fifteen years walked out on my four children and me. Life as I knew it was shattered. I buried myself deeper into depression. He delivered me from a bad relationship, but I couldn't see it because I didn't know his plan for me. Although I was at an all time low, I could yet hear a still voice calling me. This time I answered. God did not leave me, I left Him. When my life had turned upside down, I turned away. I was angry and upset with God. I didn't understand why I had to endure so much pain and struggle. I know now, it is a testimony to help others. How can you minister if you have no experiences? How can you witness God can deliver if you haven't been delivered?

God restored me and returned everything the devil stole from me. I have a new life and the world's finest gentleman as my husband. I have a new walk with the Lord. He is first in my life and He has promised to take care of the rest.

God saved my children's father; He is now preaching the gospel. We are prayer partners and friends, something we weren't before. God has given him a beautiful second chance for happiness. Now, our children have a special and unique blended family with lots of love.

God doesn't always fix things the way we think He should. That's because His way is not our way; His thoughts are not our thoughts. But when He restores, He is a God of completion.